Enjoy Playing Guitar

Time for Two

19 duets for the developing guitarist

Debbie Cracknell

MUSIC DEPARTMENT

OXFORD
UNIVERSITY PRESS

OXFORD
UNIVERSITY PRESS

Great Clarendon Street, Oxford OX2 6DP,
United Kingdom

Oxford University Press is a department of the University of Oxford.
It furthers the University's objective of excellence in research, scholarship,
and education by publishing worldwide. Oxford is a registered trade mark of
Oxford University Press in the UK and in certain other countries

First published 2013

Impression: 3

ISBN 978-0-19-339080-5

Music and text origination by
Julia Bovee
Printed in Great Britain on acid-free paper by
Halstan & Co. Ltd, Amersham, Bucks.

Contents

Preface

Time for Two is a progressive selection of duets for classical guitarists in a wide variety of styles. With pieces from the Baroque through to newly composed music, it takes in classical, folk, ragtime, and blues along the way. Technical challenges are few, allowing both parts to be played by students as well as with a teacher. The collection also provides good sight-reading practice for more experienced players.

A number of the pieces in this collection began life as guitar solos and have been arranged so that students can sample music from the well-known guitar composers before facing the technical challenges of playing these pieces as solos. Short background notes and performance tips are included for each piece, and the accompanying CD contains separate recordings of the individual guitar parts, giving players a chance to practise in preparation for playing with other guitarists. A number of slower tracks are provided so that students can build up the speed gradually for some of the faster pieces. Track 1 is a tuning track: each open string is played three times, from string 1 to string 6. Each piece has a two-bar click-track intro (including any upbeat).

Full performances of the duets are available to download from the *Enjoy Playing Guitar: Time for Two* page of www.oup.com/uk (click on the link to the Companion Website).

Debbie Cracknell, 2013

'Nothing is more beautiful than a guitar, except, possibly, two.'　　　　Frédéric Chopin

2: Guitar 1

3: Guitar 2

Prince Rupert's March

This is an old English country-dance tune from the seventeenth century. Guitar 1: at the start and end of the piece, tap the body of the guitar with the fingers, or the side of the right-hand thumb, to produce a drum-like effect.

Trad. (English)

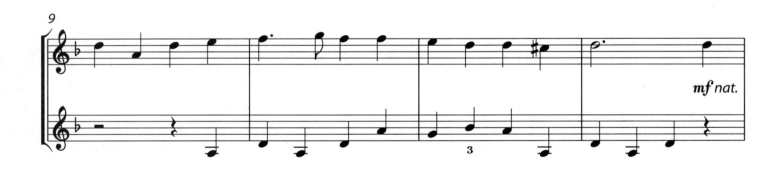

4: Guitar 1
5: Guitar 2

Waltz in G

40: Guitar 1 (practice track)
41: Guitar 2 (practice track)

This piece was originally written for solo guitar by the prolific Italian composer Ferdinando Carulli. Take it fairly fast and keep it lively in feel, making sure there is plenty of dynamic contrast for the repeats.

Ferdinando Carulli
(1770–1841)

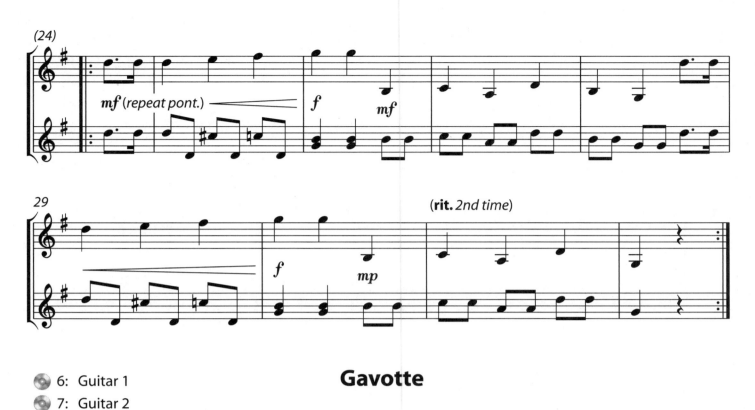

6: Guitar 1

7: Guitar 2

Gavotte

A gavotte is a type of dance, originally from France. This one was written in the Baroque period by the Italian woodwind player and composer Francesco Barsanti and was originally for recorder and continuo (keyboard). For variety, try swapping parts on the repeats.

Francesco Barsanti
(1690–1772)

8: Guitar 1
9: Guitar 2

Arkansas Traveller

42: Guitar 1 (practice track)
43: Guitar 2 (practice track)

This traditional bluegrass tune from the southern states of the USA should be played at an upbeat tempo. Notice where Guitar 2 takes over the tune, and make sure the player emphasizes these passages.

Trad. (American)

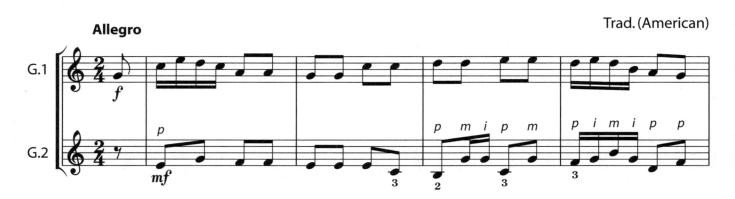

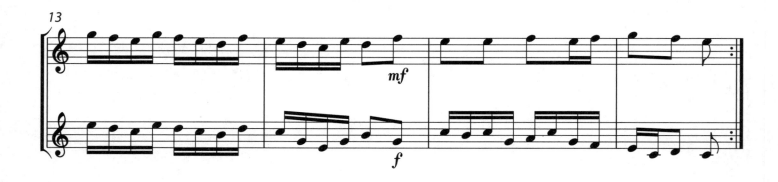

10: Guitar 1
11: Guitar 2

Allegretto

44: Guitar 1 (practice track) *
45: Guitar 2 (practice track) *

The Italian composer Mauro Giuliani wrote four *Northern Dances* for solo guitar, and the 'Allegretto' is taken from the third of these. Keep it lilting along with a dance-like feel, counting two to a bar. Play all the grace notes (*acciaccaturas*) on the beat, with a left-hand downward slur (pull-off).

Mauro Giuliani
(1781–1829)

* The click count-in for the slower practice track is in 6.

12: Guitar 1
13: Guitar 2

Marcha

46: Guitar 1 (practice track)
47: Guitar 2 (practice track)

This piece is arranged from a guitar solo by the Argentinian guitarist and composer Julio S. Sagreras. Allow the bass notes to ring on in the Guitar 2 part at bar 5 (and all similar places). In bar 38, Guitar 1 has the option to jump up the octave for the second C, as indicated by *8va*.

Julio S. Sagreras
(1879–1942)

🔘 14: Guitar 1

🔘 15: Guitar 2

Koto Music

Written towards the end of the twentieth century, 'Koto Music' is one of two pieces originally for guitar solo in a Japanese style by the British composer Carey Blyton. Guitar 2: to avoid hitting more than the required four strings at bar 4 and similar places, rest your index finger on the B string while strumming with the thumb. Both parts should allow the notes to ring on in bar 27, and in bar 28 bend the string slightly out of tune with a slow, lateral vibrato. Watch out for the sections marked *sub. p* ('suddenly soft'). In bar 27, *ad lib.* means 'take at your own speed'.

Carey Blyton
(1932–2002)

16: Guitar 1
17: Guitar 2

Yo vendo unos ojos negros

The title of this Chilean folk song translates as 'I sell black eyes'; the singer longs to escape from the gaze of a lover who has enchanted and betrayed him. Guitar 2: let the bass (thumb) notes ring on as indicated in bars 5–8 and in all similar arpeggio passages. In both parts, make sure you emphasize the accented notes in bars 15, 19, 23, and 27 to create a 3/4 feel. This alternation between 6/8 and 3/4 rhythms is characteristic of much South American music.

Trad. (Chilean)

18: Guitar 1
19: Guitar 2

Rocky Ground

Make sure you swing the quavers in this piece to give it a jazzy feel, and note the 'ground bass'—a bass line that is repeated over and over throughout. The *acciaccaturas* in bars 13 and 20 are played on the beat with a slide to the main note. The very high slide, D to E in bar 20, is found on frets 10 to 12 on the first string.

Debbie Cracknell

20: Guitar 1
21: Guitar 2

Fiesta Parade

This piece allows you to practise the guitarist's favourite chords of Am and E. Guitar 2: play 'tambora' where indicated—hit the strings very near the bridge with the side of the right-hand thumb while holding down the chord. At bar 21, strum the chords in the direction of the arrows, continuing the strumming pattern of the previous bar when it says *simile* in bar 22.

Debbie Cracknell

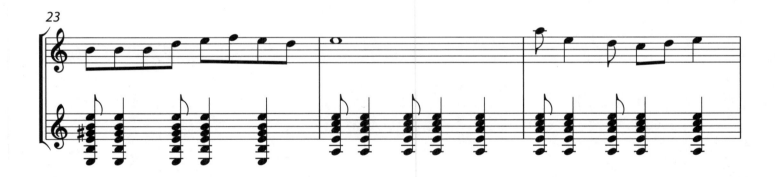

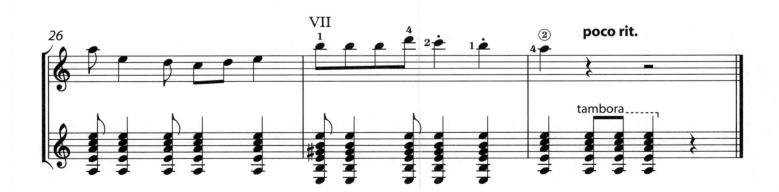

22: Guitar 1
23: Guitar 2

La Tarara

This is a popular song in Spain about a beautiful girl called Tarara. It should feel gentle and flowing in style, so make sure the strummed chords in the introduction don't get any louder than *mp*.

Anon. (Spanish)

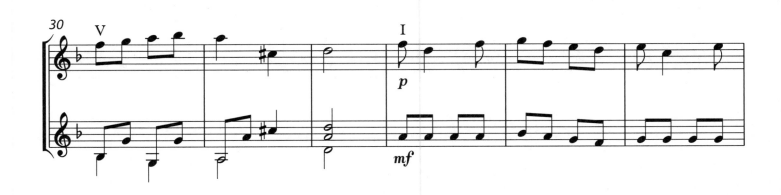

24: Guitar 1
25: Guitar 2

Jingle Bell Rock

Since its original recording in 1957 by Bobby Helms, 'Jingle Bell Rock' has been covered by many singers and is still one of the most popular Christmas songs, especially in the USA. Play it at a steady swing throughout.

Joe Beal (1900–1967) &
Jim Boothe (1917–1976)

26: Guitar 1
27: Guitar 2

Waltz in G

This waltz by the Spanish guitarist Daniel Fortea was originally written as a guitar solo, and it provides Guitar 1 with some good opportunities for playing in the higher positions. Keep the piece moving gently and make the melody sing out, perhaps with a little vibrato. Guitar 2 should use free stroke throughout, and take all notes at the fourth fret in bars 34–5. In the original solo, bars 1–32 and 33–48 are repeated before moving on to the D.C.

Daniel Fortea
(1878–1953)

28: Guitar 1

29: Guitar 2

La Cumparsita

This famous tango was written in 1917 by Uruguayan composer Gerardo Matos Rodríguez, and the title translates as 'The little parade'. Guitar 2 could use a *rasgueado* at bars 2, 17, and 32, rather than a straight strum. To play these chords *rasgueado*, strum across the strings with the backs of the right-hand fingernails one after the other, beginning with the little finger. The mordents in the Guitar 1 part are optional.

Gerardo Matos Rodríguez
(1897–1948)

D.S. al Fine

🔘 30: Guitar 1
🔘 31: Guitar 2

Bourrée

A bourrée is a type of French dance that was popular in the seventeenth and eighteenth centuries. This one is taken from the first suite by Robert de Visée for solo guitar, written at the end of the seventeenth century. A little emphasis on the first beat of each bar will give the piece a dance-like feel. Strum the chords in the Guitar 2 part in the direction of the arrows, using *p* or *i* as indicated.

Robert de Visée
(*c*.1655–*c*.1732)

32: Guitar 1

33: Guitar 2

Latin Nocturne

Guitar 2: tune string 6 to D as indicated—you will only need to play this string as an open note. A nocturne is a 'night piece', so aim to give this a gentle and lazy feel. Guitar 1 should use vibrato on the tune where possible.

Debbie Cracknell

34: Guitar 1
35: Guitar 2

Felicity Rag

48: Guitar 1 (practice track)
49: Guitar 2 (practice track)

This piece was composed at the beginning of the twentieth century by the popular ragtime pianist Scott Joplin and his friend Scott Hayden. Try playing the bass line slightly detached to enhance the character of the rag. The Guitar 1 part can be optionally played an octave higher in bar 12, as indicated.

Scott Joplin (1867–1917) &
Scott Hayden (1882–1915)

36: Guitar 1
37: Guitar 2

Over the Rainbow

This song featured in the 1939 movie *The Wizard of Oz* and has become a popular standard over the years. Play it expressively and use vibrato on the tune where possible, especially where Guitar 1 is in fifth position. Bars 25–6 and 29–30 should be played across strings 1 and 2 in the Guitar 1 part.

Harold Arlen
(1905–1986)

38: Guitar 1
39: Guitar 2

Gran Vals

This piece is arranged from a much longer solo by the Spanish guitarist and composer Francisco Tárrega, and was originally written in A major. The *acciaccatura* in the Guitar 1 part should be on the beat; play the B on fret 4, string 3, and slide immediately to fret 7 to produce the D. (You may recognize this tune as a popular mobile phone ringtone!)

Francisco Tárrega
(1852–1909)